Wolves
For Kids
Amazing Animal Books
for Young Readers

by John Davidson and Virginia Fidler

Read More Amazing Animal Books

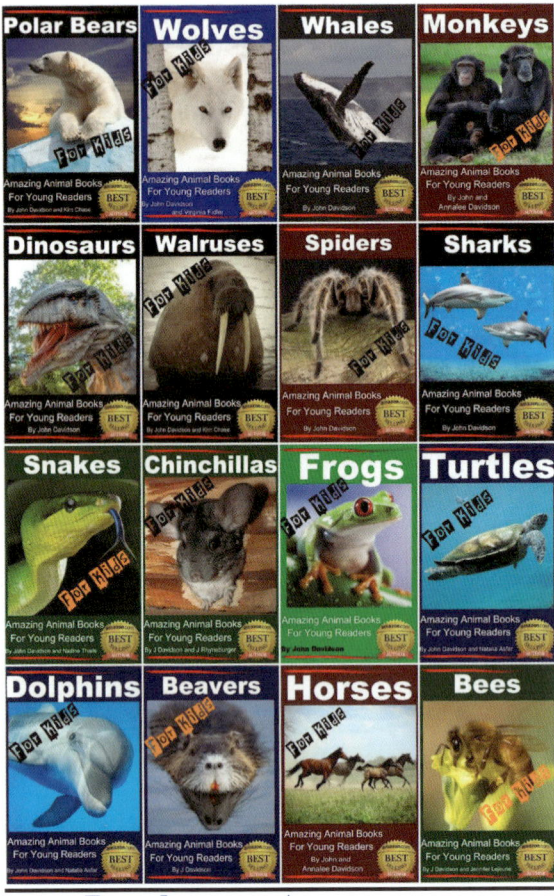

Purchase at Amazon.com

Table of Contents

1. Introduction

The wolf belongs to the canine family. In America, the gray wolf, also called a timber wolf, is the largest member of that family. This majestic animal is the ancestor of the dogs we keep as pets, and he is a cousin to the coyote and the fox.

Gray wolves can survive in most climates, although they prefer the cold. They have roamed the Americas from Alaska to Mexico since the last Ice Age. By 1960, hunting reduced the wolf population to 300 in the lower 48 states, most of which lived in Minnesota and Michigan. Some of the wolves were placed in Yellowstone Park, where they are able to breed successfully. Today, there are 4,000 wolves roaming the Rockies and Northern states. Some farmers are upset that the wolves are stealing their chickens and young livestock, but that's what wolves do. They hunt to survive and eat.

2. 10 Facts About Wolves

1. Wolves are social and very loyal animals.

2. Collectively, wolves are known as Canis lupus.

3. Wolves live in packs and each pack usually comprises of 4-6 wolves.

4. Wolves communicate with each other through sounds. They bark, grunt and growl.

5. Gray wolves are the most common type of wolves. The gray wolves have very good communication skills.

6. They are found to be more active during the night time.

7. The wolves are found to run on their toes. This enables them to be active and sharp runners.

8. The wolf pups are born blind and deaf. They weigh only about 1 pound at the time of their birth.

9. Wolves have small webs between their toes which enable them to swim up to a distance of 6 miles.

10. The adult male in a pack is termed as the "Alpha Male" and the adult female is termed as the "Alpha Female".

3. Wolves as Pets

Wolves are beautiful animals, and they look so much like our pet dogs, it can be difficult not to confuse the two species. It's easy to want to give a wolf a hug. There are people who try to turn a wolf into a pet, and that's a very bad idea. Wolves may learn to live among humans, especially if they've been raised by humans since they were a pup, but they don't lose their natural and wild instincts.

Wolf © JackF - Fotolia.com

Wolves should not be kept in captivity. Dog pups and wolf pups act pretty much the same when they are young. As they mature, however, wolves will exhibit much of the behavior of wolves in the wild.

Dogs and wolves may come from a common ancestor, but it has taken 10,000 years for the dog to be what we know today – man's best friend. During that same time, wolves have lived on their own, defended themselves, and taken care of themselves. That behavior is bred into them. So try to imagine this independent wolf living with people and doing what people tell him to.

After 10,000 years, the dog will happily fetch your slippers. The wolf will rip them apart.

In the wild, wolves want to become alpha or the leader. It's in their nature. If they were a pet, they would respect you as the alpha, but they would continually challenge you. It's in a wolf's nature to want to be alpha, no matter where he lives. He will become hard, if not impossible, to control.

Wolves are beautiful and smart – if they are allowed to be wolves. If you try to domesticate a wolf, it won't work. Wolves are territorial pack animals by their very nature. They respect the alpha, and with a wolf, you might be the alpha, for a while. But like in the wild, the alpha can be dethroned and killed. It's what wolves do. And they belong in the wild, with their pack.

4. Do Wolves Hurt People?

Probably no piece of literature has given the wolf as bad a reputation as Little Red Riding Hood, a story about a wolf and a little girl. The wolf is mean and nasty, and that is the way many people think of the wolf.

© hammett79 - Fotolia.com

The fact is, wolves are scared of humans. They will hunt very large animals, but they try to stay out of sight of people. They understand that humans have guns and that guns can kill. When wolves feel threatened by people, they will take a stance. Their eyes look angry, and their lips are pulled back in a snarl. All they want is a chance to retreat without getting hurt or killed.
Wolf attacks on humans are extremely rare, and then, most likely the attack is a defensive act.

5. How Intelligent Are Wolves?

Are wolves smarter than a fifth-grader? No, they're not. It's not easy to judge a wolf's brain power, but studies indicate that wolves can remember certain things, make associations, and learn. For example, when the bison was being exterminated, the wolves connected the noise of the gunshots with danger and remained out of sign until the hunter was out of sight. When wolves in Montana were killed from planes, they learned to associate planes with danger and stayed away from open areas and would wait until the hunters had abandoned the bison carcasses before feeding on them.

Wolves can be trained to do a few things, but they are not as trainable as our pet dogs. They don't respond to negative and positive stimuli, such as giving a treat to a dog who has mastered a command and withholding the treat when the dog has not.

Gray Wolf © nialat - Fotolia.com

Wolves may respond better to hand signals than to verbal commands. The reason is unknown, it but may have something to do with the fact that wolves communicate a great deal by physical movements. A biologist tried to train wolves to become sled dogs. The wolves learned to pull in a straight line, but they argued over space. Once they were tired, they simply ignored the verbal commands.

6. Do Wolves Communicate?

Many people think that writing and reading are the only forms of communication. Animals do not read or write, but they do communicate in various ways.

The rules of the pack, as determined by the alpha couple, is broadcast through body language. The first rule demands that the pack recognizes the alpha couple as being in charge.

Wolves © loflo - Fotolia.com

Alphas hold their tail high and stand straight do communicate their dominant position. Less high-ranking wolves exhibit their submissive behavior by keeping their tail and head lowered. Another way to show submission is for the wolf to lay on his or her back, leaving his body unprotected.

Lower ranking wolves cannot mate, so they can get upset at the alpha couple for mating. Sometimes, a beta or omega wolf takes control of his or her life, leaves the pack and moves into a pack with a missing alpha. If possible, the newcomer will try and take the old alpha's place or perhaps kills another alpha and keep its mate.

When a wolf is angry, he straightens his ears and shows his teeth. A confused or suspicious wolf with hold the ears back and squint. Fear will make a wolf hold his ears flat against his head.

Obviously, the ears are an important communication devise for wolves. One of the most important communication methods for wolves is their remarkable sense of smell. They are able to smell 100 times better than you or I. Wolves use urine to mark a particular territory. Any wolf from another pack immediately knows that another wolf came here first. Members of a pack can recognize the urine of individual pack members.

Wolves will also use urine to scent mark food caches that have been exhausted. By marking an empty cache, they will not waste time digging for food that isn't there.
Needless to say, a wolf can smell food or an enemy at a considerable distance.

Of course, their sense of smell also tells them when food or enemies are near.
Wolves use sound to communicate. A bark is a warning. A combination of bark and howl is a threat in defense of the territory. A whimper is a submissive sound toward a more dominant member of the pack. A nursing mother may also whimper to signify her readiness to nurse her pups.

A growl is a warning sign used against predators or a less dominant wolf, a canine equivalent of, "Don't mess with me."
A howl is intended to be heard from afar; think of it as canine telephone. A howl can be heard up to six miles away in a forest, and ten miles in an area with no trees.

Howling can be a cry for the pack to get together, and it can reveal the location of a lone member to the rest of the pack, a canine "Here I am!" A chorus of howls can be a warning to other, non-member, wolves to go away.

7. How Do Wolves Hunt?

The wolf is considered to be one of the best and fiercest hunters. They are able to stalk a prey and they can successfully overpower a prey that is 10 times bigger than they are. One of the reasons they are such powerful hunters is that they work as a team.

They work together, and they keep practicing so that their skills keep improving. Like an athlete who continuously practices and becomes better at his sports, the wolf works hard at improving his hunting skills. When the time comes for a hunt, they are as prepared as an Olympian.

pack of european grey wolves © *Photohunter - Fotolia.com*

Both male and females hunt, and the female is an important part of the process. Because she is smaller, she is swifter than the male and is able to reach fast speeds. The one female who does not participate in a hunt is the alpha female. Her contribution to the pack is to provide it with the necessary pups, and she is too important for the pack to risk her becoming injured. She does watch and makes sure that the other females do their part properly.

One reason this teamwork is critical to a successful hunt is that wolves hunt animals that are much larger than they are, such as caribou, deer, elk, and moose. Obviously, not every hunt against such large prey is successful, so they eat when they can to fill up.

Because of their thick, rich fur, wolfs prefer hunting in winter, when it is cooler. During that time of year, it's also easier to follow a prey's prints in the snow. Hunting is an exciting event, and the wolves approach it with their tails wagging. Sometimes, the pups get caught up in all of the excitement and follow the pack, which means the little ones can spoil and ruin a good hunt by getting in the way.

Wolves like to the hunt at night for the same reason they hunt in the winter – the temperature is cooler. While they may encounter a prey by accident, usually they act upon their sense of smell or hunt by tracking. When they sense a prey, they split up for maximum efficiency. They hide in tall grass and climb ridges for a better view. They also observe a herd in order to single out a weak member.

Wolves can bring down a buffalo that is weak or too slow to remain with his group. A weak prey will show signs of his weakness by the way he moves or by giving off the scent if an infection. Wolves can track a herd by the smell of its food prints. Because many of the wolves' prey are incredible runners, the pack attacks immediately. Wolves chase their prey until it is tired, and they have been seen chasing deer for as far as 13 miles. That is how they are able to overpower a prey much larger than they are.

The fact is, however, despite being a skillful hunter, most of the wolves end up with their prey escaping.

8. How Wolves Live

Wolves are social animals who enjoy each other's company. They live and hunt in groups called packs. These wolf packs usually include less than ten wolves and are families lead by the alpha wolves and their young pups. Cousins sometimes join and leave a pack at random, increasing the size of a pack to up to 30 wolves. The only ones allowed to mate and breed are the alpha male and alpha female. Wolves who are not members of the pack are rarely tolerated inside the pack's territory. Some territories can spread out to 1,600 square miles.

© *fotografie4you.eu - Fotolia.com*

If one alpha is injured or deposed, his mate may continue to rule the pack, if he or she is strong enough. If the alpha is deposed by common consensus, the deposition may result in the alpha's death.

Alphas become alphas by demonstrating their ability to dominate and control the rest of the pack. If a younger upstart challenges an existing alpha, they will have repeated fights until one of them is considered the winner. The ruling alpha wins the right to mate.

The Beta Wolves are a kind of second string, the lieutenants of the wolf world. They may occasionally challenge the alpha and try to mate with the alpha female. A beta is the most likely wolf to replace the current alpha.

The omega wolf is the least powerful and can get picked on by others. They may be considered the nerds of the wolf world. This occasional harassment by alphas and betas is a socially accepted way for the stronger wolves to handle their natural aggression. Some omegas are able to fight their way up to beta, and perhaps alpha level.

The only parents in the pack are the alpha male and alpha female. They lead the pack on hunts, determine where they will live, and mark their chosen territory. The alpha couple is not necessarily the strongest paid, but is the pair with the best decision-making ability and the most strength. They tend to be the smartest in the group.

Prior to giving birth, the alpha female will chose a den in which she will raise her pups. The den has to be close to water. The den can be a space by sheltered by rocks, a log that is hollow and large enough, or beneath a rock overhang. The entrance to the den can be up the twenty-six inches wide. The entrance leads to a tunnel that extends to a birthing chamber for the alpha female. Several generations of wolves can use the same den. A wolf will give birth to about 5 to 7 pups, but perhaps half of them won't survive for one year. The female and her pups will remain in the den until the pups are old enough to venture out.

At birth, a wolf pup weighs one pound, just a little less than a polar bear pup. They grow quickly, and it'll weigh up to 20 pounds within two months. By the end of their first year, wolf pups are the size of their parents.

Gray wolves have pups once a year. When the alpha female gives birth, all of the females in the pack help her. The pups stay inside the den for the first few weeks. At that stage, they are deaf and blind, and they depend on their mother for nourishment.

When the pups can hear and see, they start to play outside of the den. Older females siblings may look after them while the alpha female hunts with the other adult pack members. While the pups play, they chew bones, which sharpens their teeth and prepares them for adulthood. The pup is mature by the age of two. At that point, the pack usually moves on in search of food somewhere else.

The pack can travel up to 30 miles each day when they are tracking food. Gray wolves will hunt antelopes, deer, moose, goats, and elk. They'll eat mice and squirrels if they have to.

The body of gray wolves is designed for hunting. Their strong canine teeth and molars can slash meat and crunch bones. The feet on their front leg have five toes, and the feet on the hind legs have four toes. The gray wolf has a large stomach, and a large wolf can eat over 20 pounds of meat at one time. That comes in handy, since wolves frequently fast for days until thy hunt down their next prey.

Mature gray wolves use 42 teeth that have very specific functions. The fangs are used for gripping. The wolf uses the incisors for tearing off small bits of meat.

If there is abundant prey, gray wolves might kill it and leave the carcass for other animals, or they may bury their kill for some other time.

9. Re-instating the Wolf in Yellowstone Park

Once the gray wolf came close to extinction, scientists noticed that everything in nature works in harmony. By eliminating the gray wolf, hunters were creating an imbalance in the ecosystem of the Northwestern part of the United States.

When men hunted down the gray wolf, the land on which they roamed lost the water crucial for other species to survive. There were fewer wetlands, creeks, and streams. The reason is simple. When the elks, one of the wolf's favorite prey, no longer had to worry about being hunted, they moved freely in the open and started to eat willow and seedlings before they become mature.

With the decline of the willow tree, beavers, who used the willow to build their homes and dams, could no longer build, so they went someplace else. The dams created the wetlands, and without the dams, there were no wetlands. This affected much of the fish and bugs living in the ponds. As Yellowstone dried up, species began to disappear. In nature, everything and everyone depends on the rest. What affects one affects all.

This explains one of the major reasons why the wolf was re-instated into Yellowstone in early 1995. Wildlife representatives from the United States and Canada captured several of them and let them lose in the park. This initial group of wolves was soon joined by 17 more wolves. By 2011, there were 98 wolves in Yellowstone. There has been a slight decline since that year.

10. History of the Gray Wolf

The gray wolf lived on the North American continent 18,000 years ago, long before the Inuit and Native Americans crossed the land bridge connecting Alaska and Russia
.
Some people believe that the domesticated dog is a descendant of an early wolf species.

Large Female Gray Wolf

The earliest ancestors of today's wolf lived around 30 million years ago. The fox is also descendants from this common ancestor. Around 7 to 9 million years ago, the more recent ancestor of the wolf became a separate species. Another species was created when the wolf split from the coyote.

The species that remained, called Canis lupis, greatly resembles today's wolf. Scientists have discovered these facts by examining fossils and old bones, and noting the changes in skull and teeth size, and bones.

Approximately 500,000 to one million wolves shared this land with the Native Americans and ate much of the humans leftovers. The wolf is a part of much Native American folklore, and many tribes believed that their ancestors were wolves who turned into humans.

11. What Does the Gray Wolf Look Like?

The gray wolf is a powerful animal that has a slanting rib cage and back. Male wolves weigh about 95 pounds, while female wolves weigh around 80 pounds. Male wolves have reached a weight of 120 pounds. The color of their thick, coarse fur can range from gray to black. A few gray wolves have all-white fur.

Gray Wolf Mother with Pups

The gray wolf looks like a German shepherd, with a larger head and longer legs. It's the long legs that enables the gray wolf to move at a good speed and step through the snow that frequently covers his habitat and domain for at least part of the year. They also have a bushy tail and small ears. When he walks, the wolf moves one paw precisely in front of the other, making for an easy and comfortable pace.

Females wolves are slightly smaller, with shorter legs and less shoulder muscles than the males. Females may be smaller, but in terms of rank within the pack, they are the equal of male wolves and get to boss less powerful male members of the pack around.

Wolves are designed to live in cool climate. Their fur is very dense and thick, and some of the hair is shed during warmer weather. The paws maintain a temperature that is lower than body temperature but above freezing. This allows the gray wolf to walk on ice and snow. They can be quite comfortable at 10 degrees below freezing.

12. Hunting the Gray Wolf

Native Americans stalked and hunted the gray wolf when they stole from their food supply. Many tribes, such as the Cherokee, were afraid that if they unnecessarily killed a gray wolf, the rest of the pack would return for revenge. Apaches training to become warriors would kill wolves and other prey as a test of strength and daring. No one killed a gray wolf without a reason.

The relationship between wolf and man changed drastically when the European settlers arrived in America. Since wolves hunt farm animals, the settlers were angry when they lost their livestock to a wolf attack. To protect their farms, the settlers felt they needed to kill all of the wolves they could. The settlers were so determined to rid their farms of wolves that by the mid of the 19th century, the once plentiful wolves were close to extinction in the eastern area of the United States.

Wolf Through Glass at West Yellowstone © feather ridge images - Fotolia.com

Before the Civil War, people hunted mainly for food or to rid themselves of dangerous prey. Following the Civil War, however, many British immigrants moved to the new continent, and they brought their love of hunting with them.

Hunting down the gray wolf became a sport. The one who killed the most won a trophy. Some might consider this the old-fashioned equivalent of a violent video game. The killing and extermination of the wolves, however, were real.

13. The Ethiopian Wolf

The Ethiopian wolf lives in the forest of the Ethiopian Highland and is the only member of the canine family living in Africa. The land is dry and harsh, with bits of shrubbery and bleak mountain tops. The Ethiopian wolf feeds on the rodents that are unique to the area.

They have colorful and red and white fur. The Ethiopian wolf is the rarest and more extinct of wolves, with only 550 remaining on these isolated mountain ranges, although some have put the number as low as 400.

Simien wolf, Ethiopian Highlands

The main continued threat to the Ethiopian wolf's survival is that farmer are moving up the mountains to tilt the soil, thereby threatening the Ethiopian wolf's habitat and way of life. It is on the Endangered Species list.

The Ethiopian wolf resembles the American coyote more than it does the gray wolf. It has a flat skull and a long, narrow face. Males can weigh up to 45 pounds, and females weigh up to 30 pounds. Its fur is short and thick, since the temperature can get low. The area around the belly and chest is white, while the rest of the fur is a reddish, ginger color. There is a white streak by the throat.

When a female is ready to breed, her fur turns a shade of yellow. Like all wolves, the Ethiopian wolf is very social and lives in a pack with family members.

Like the gray wolf, the Ethiopian wolf's pack has a clearly established hierarchy. They do, however search for rodent food alone and eat by themselves.

They may hunt together if the prey is a larger animal.

The biggest threat to the Ethiopian wolf is disease and habitat infringement. Ethiopia is working on programs to monitor diseases and protect the small area that is the home of the Ethiopian wolf.

14. The Arctic Wolf

The arctic wolf is relative of the gray wolf, and their habitats are among the most unfriendly and unwelcoming terrain in existence. At the arctic, the temperature tends to stay at around 33 degrees below freezing. The ground never thaws and stays frozen throughout the year. The arctic region extends from northern Canada to northern Greenland and parts of Alaska. It is possible that the arctic wolf lived as far south as North America a few million years ago, during the last glacial period.

Artic Wolf © bmaynard - Fotolia.com

The arctic wolf is so isolated that he doesn't come in much contact with humans, so there is little chance of him being hunted. He's the only wolf who is not in danger of becoming extinct. The only genuine threat to the arctic wolf is the severe weather and the lack of food.

The hardy arctic wolf is one of the rare animals that is able to survive under such brutal conditions. To be able to tolerate such frigid weather, the arctic wolf is smaller than his cousin, the gray wolf, and has shorter ears, legs, and muzzle at to lessen the effect of the icy environment, where is remains totally dark for up to five month a year. The all-white coat, of course, is thick enough so that the arctic wolf can handle the cold.

Arctic wolves are usually smaller than gray wolves, and also have little ears, a short muzzle, and shorter legs. They usually live in packs. They are often all white with thick fur, Their fur gets thick during the winter and they shed or loose it during the summer. Their coat keeps them warm and the white color helps them hide in the snow.
Like all wolves, the arctic wolf is a member of a family pack which includes the alpha parent couple and their offspring, and everyone takes care of the little ones. In order to mate, the mature young offspring leave the home to find a mate somewhere else. In the wild, wolves live up to ten years.

Arctic wolves hunt in packs and track down caribous and muskoxen. They also go after seals and any other small animals in the region. They do not run very quickly, but their natural stamina allows them to tire out their prey. When they catch their food, they eat everything, including the bones. In the arctic, nothing goes to waste. They eat up to 20 pounds at one sitting, and regurgitate meat to feed their pups.

Like other wolves, the female arctic wolf tries to raise her pups in a safe den. However, when she can't dig through the snow, she'll find a cave and some shallow indentation in the ground to shelter her pups.

Due to lack of natural prey, arctic wolves need to roam far for food, sometimes up to 1000 square miles. They go south for the winter to hunt the caribou.

15. Himalayan Wolf

Until recently, the Himalayan wolf was somewhat unknown to humans. There are approximately 300 Himalayan wolves left, living in the remoteness of the Himalayan Mountains. Until a few years ago, the Himalayan wolf was believed to be a relative of the gray wolf.

However, the entire wolf species is distantly related to the dog family, and the Himalayan wolf is genetically not a dog. The Himalayan wolf and the dog became divided as a species around 800,000 years ago. In 2009, the Himalayan received a new classification, Canis Himalayensis.

The Himalayan wolf is thought to be the oldest representative of any known animal in existence today. This would make his lineage extremely valuable. However, although they are on the Endangered Species list, very little is being done to protect the few numbers of Himalayan wolves left. India has created a breeding program for a group of 30 Himalayan wolves, but much more is needed to save this unique species.

Despite the Himalayan wolf's status as endangered, he is still being hunted. It is possible that soon, there will be no Himalayan wolf in existence.

16. Tundra Wolf

The tundra wolf, Canis Lupus Albus, is a part of the gray wolf family. They are found in Asia and Europe and also by the Arctic. They are almost as big as the gray wolf, measuring 7 feet nose to tail. They can weigh up to 150 pounds, all though some can weigh as much as 220 pounds. They can grow up to 38 inches high.

Their coat is a mix of white and grey, which is an excellent for hiding in the snowy north. Its fur is thick, fluffy, and the tundra wolf is hunted for its pelt in Canada and Russia.

Tundra wolf (Canis lupus arctos) on the snow © *meoita - Fotolia.com*

The tundra is a northern region with a frozen layer just beneath th surface of the earth.

Tundra wolves live in packs and preys on reindeer, caribou and hares. Unlike other wolves, tundra wolves don't remai place and don't form territories.

They follow their major food source, caribou herds, south during the winter. This strongly affects the caribou population; between 1944 to 1954, the tundra wolves hunted and killed 75,000 caribous. This then affects the Nenets people, who need the caribou in order to survive. When tundra wolves cannot get enough caribou to eat, the female has less pups, and the tundra wolf population decreases.

Since there is plenty of land in the northern tundra, the tundra wolves are in no danger of losing their habitat. However, they stalk the reindeer farms for food, and the farmers try to shoot them off their property.

17. Red Wolf

The red wolf, known as carnis rufus, is the only member of the canine family who prefers living in warm, balmy weather. A native of America, he prefers the sunny temperatures of the southeast. Although zoologists are unsure of the red wolf's ancestry, they believe he may be a mix of coyote and the gray wolf. He weighs anywhere from 35 to 50 pounds and has coarse red fur. As with all wolves, the male is somewhat larger than the female.

Red Wolf

At one time, the red wolf roamed the southwest with abundance. When the settlers built homes and farms, the wolves attacked the livestock, and the number of red wolves began to decrease. The government joined in hunting the red wolf, and today, there are none left in Texas and parts of Louisiana, where they once were so plentiful.

The red wolf was re-introduced (just like the gray wolf) in North Carolina in the late 1980's, and there are 505 red wolves in that state. They may be the only red wolves left in the United States, except for those living in zoos.

The red wolves will only go hunting at night, and they don't hunt in packs. Instead, they go out alone or with their mate. Red wolves hunt small animals, such as rabbits, which they capture with their back legs and their paws.

The red wolf became a separate species from the gray wolf and the coyote about 200,000 to 300,000 years ago. They thrived in all of the United States, from Maine to Florida and north up to Canada. For the most part, they liked living near rivers and swamps, which exist in abundance in the southeast.

About the Authors

Virginia Fidler has published two adult novels, and this is her first children's book. She has worked at a zoo in Chicago and fell in love with the animals. Virginia greatly enjoys seeing children learn about the world around them and hopes that children who read this book will learn to appreciate the beauty of animals as much as she does.

John Davidson has written, co-authored and published over 50 books and sold over 100,000 books in the last couple years. He is an educator with over 25 years' experience in the classroom. He is a new grandfather who started Amazing Animal Books to give his grandkids educational opportunities to read about the animals around the world.

Read More Amazing Animal Books

Purchase at Amazon.com
Website http://AmazingAnimalBooks.com

Join our newsletter and receive
Amazing Animal Fact Sheets and
Get new books to review as soon as they come out

Newsletter Sign Up

This book is published by

JD-Biz Corp
P O Box 374
Mendon, Utah 84325
http://www.jd-biz.com/

Read more books from John Davidson

Amazon.com Author Link
Over 50 Books and over 100,000 copies Downloaded

Printed in Great Britain
by Amazon